Piano Solo

WAR HORSE

MUSIC FROM THE MOTION PICTURE SOUNDTRACK

COMPOSED BY JOHN WILLIAMS

ISBN 978-1-4584-2359-7

HAL•LEONARD®
CORPORATION
7777 W. BLUEMOUND RD. P.O. BOX 13819 MILWAUKEE, WI 53213

D1477904

Visit Hal Leonard Online at
www.halleonard.com

CONTENTS

4   Dartmoor, 1912

10   The Auction

14   Bringing Joey Home, and Bonding

19   Learning The Call

27   Seeding, and Horse vs. Car

34   Plowing

43   The Death Of Topthorn

46   Remembering Emilie, and Finale

49   The Homecoming

DARTMOOR, 1912

Composed by
JOHN WILLIAMS

Moderately

With pedal

Moderately fast

THE AUCTION

Composed by
JOHN WILLIAMS

Moderately, steadily

mp

With pedal

BRINGING JOEY HOME, AND BONDING

Composed by
JOHN WILLIAMS

Moderately slow, deliberately

*Continue holding note with L.H. while playing melody with R.H.

Moderately slow, freely

With motion, expressively

mf

rit. e dim.

LEARNING THE CALL

Composed by
JOHN WILLIAMS

Moderately, expressively

mf

With pedal

rit.

Faster, more steadily

Slightly faster, in 4

SEEDING, AND HORSE VS. CAR

Composed by
JOHN WILLIAMS

Moderately slow, expressively

Slightly slower

Moderately, in 1

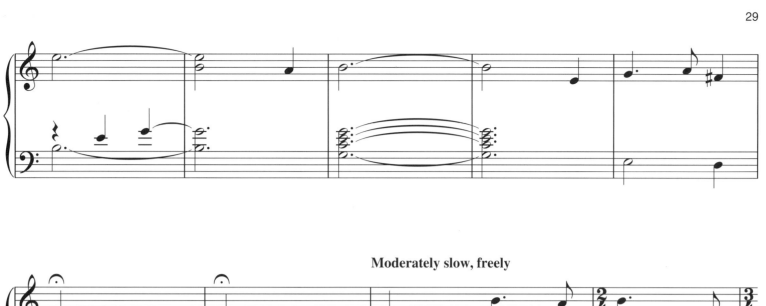

Moderately slow, freely

Moderately fast, expressively

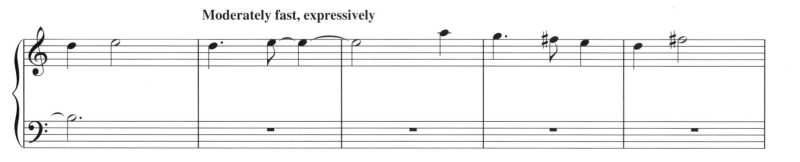

NWM

33

PLOWING

Composed by
JOHN WILLIAMS

Moderately fast

With pedal

Slightly faster, expressively

rall.

Tempo I

Tempo I

THE DEATH OF TOPTHORN

Composed by
JOHN WILLIAMS

Slowly, expressively

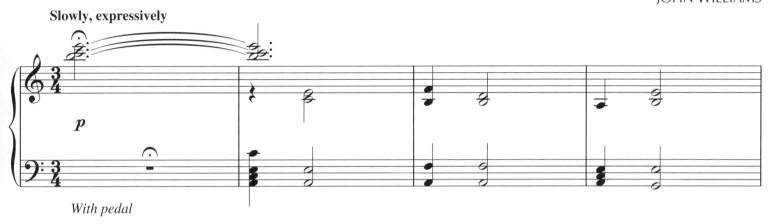

With pedal

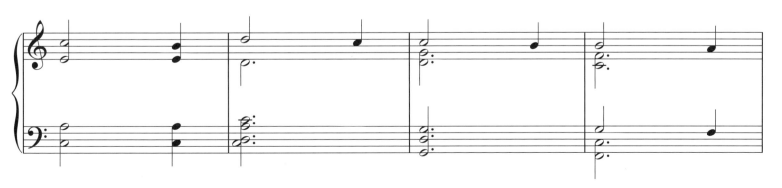

44

REMEMBERING EMILIE, AND FINALE

Composed by
JOHN WILLIAMS

Moderately, expressively

With pedal

THE HOMECOMING

Composed by
JOHN WILLIAMS

Moderately fast, in 2

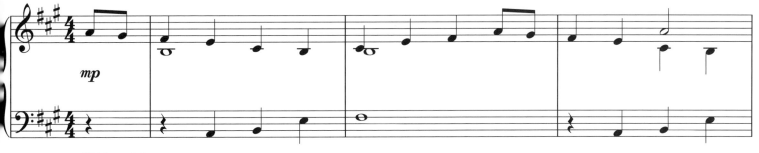

mp

With pedal

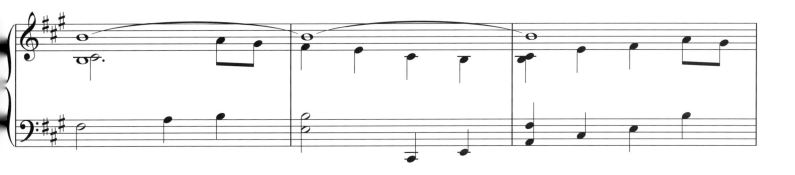

Slightly faster, freely